MAX HODES had ambitions to be a comedy script-writer, but he wasn't tall enough. He says the jokes in his book are not so much sick as slightly under the weather.

Max is a Scots journalist whose 'Chatalong with Max' column is required reading for over two million readers of the *Daily Record*, Scotland's biggest-selling daily newspaper.

He was prompted to compile this book after hearing of the little old lady trying to cross a busy road, who was helped over by a turbaned Sikh. *'Many thanks for your help,'* she said gratefully, *'and I hope your head gets better.'* That, says Max, was the Sikh joke that started it all.

LORNE BROWN, who did the drawings, is strips editor of the *Daily Record*. Among the Futura books he has illustrated are three compiled by Max Hodes: *The Official Scottish Joke Book*, *The World's Worst Joke Book*, and *The Official English, Irish and Scottish Joke Book*.

D1423665

Also in this series:

Max Hodes

The Official
Sick Joke Book

Illustrated by Lorne Brown

Macdonald Futura Publishers

A Futura Book

First published in Great Britain by
Macdonald Futura Publishers in 1980

Copyright © Max Hodes 1980

Illustrations copyright © Lorne Brown 1980

ISBN 0 7088 1931 1

Filmset, printed and bound in Great Britain
by Hazell Watson & Viney Ltd,
Aylesbury, Bucks

Macdonald Futura Publishers Ltd
Paulton House
8 Shepherdess Walk
London N1 7LW

'Have you a last request?' the priest asked the man in the electric chair.
'Just one, Father,' came the reply.
'And what's that, my son?'
'Hold my hand.'

Then there was the mortician's wife who sued for divorce. She complained her husband kept bringing his work home with him.

Seen on the back of a car:
'Sorry, no hand signals.
I am a convicted Arab shoplifter.'

Hear about the Harley Street doctor who's making so much money he no longer needs to operate on every patient?

Famous last words:
'This'll be the best home brew yet.'

'When I die, I want to be cremated,' said the man to his wife.
'That would be just like you,' she replied, 'to go and leave ashes all over the house.'

From a shop window:
'For sale, mahogany wardrobe with four drawers, three shelves and ample hanging space for man.'

'Grandad, do an impression of a frog.'
'Why do you want me to do that?'
'Well, every time I ask Mum for money, she says she won't have any till you croak.'

Notice in an undertakers:
'Funerals. Parking for clients only.'

Dad didn't like me . . . when they took me to be christened, he threw a depth charge at the font.

– Les Dawson

Erected to the memory of
JOHN McFARLANE
drown'd in the Water of Leith
by a few affectionate friends

A man was being led to the gallows in a
thunderstorm.
'Terrible weather for it,' he remarked to the
hangman.
'You should worry,' replied the hangman. 'I've got
to walk back in this.'

Good news about the man who swallowed a stick of
dynamite. He's recovering in Wards 3, 7 and 10 of
Westminster Hospital.

1st cannibal: 'Am I late for dinner?'
2nd cannibal: 'Yes, everybody's eaten.'

Then there was the psychiatrist with a double couch
for patients with a split personality.

Just before the executioner pulled the switch, the Irishman in the electric chair started laughing.
'What's so funny?' asked the executioner.
'Sure, they went and got the wrong fella – it wasn't me at all!'

Hear about the World Masochism Centre? It has big signs all over it saying how wonderful it is . . . but no doors.

El Al pilot: 'Good morning, this is your captain. I hope you have a wonderful trip. If we have any trouble flying over water, the lifebelts are under your seats. And if you have to put them on – wear them in good health.'

'I heard you just bought your mother-in-law a Jaguar.'
'That's right.'
'I thought you didn't like her?'
'I know what I'm doing – it's bitten her twice already.'

Bumper sticker:
Support mental health or I'll kill you!

'Dad, are you sure this is the right way to learn to swim?'
'Shut up and get back in the sack.'

A man listed the cost of erecting a tombstone over his wife's grave as a charitable contribution.
'Perhaps you could explain this,' asked the Inland Revenue man.
'Well,' said the man, 'in all the years we were married, my wife never did anything for me, so I look on the erection of her tombstone as an act of charity.'

Pilot to control tower: 'Am out of fuel six hundred miles over the Atlantic. Urgently request instructions.'
Control tower to pilot: 'Repeat after me. Our Father, who art in heaven . . .'

'The police want a tall handsome man in his twenties for assaults on women.'
'What's the pay like?'

Sign in car:
Give blood. Play rugby.

'I went out fishing with my wife yesterday.'
'Lucky you – I'm still using worms.'

A man took his dog to the vet and asked him to cut off its tail.
'Why do you want me to do that?' asked the vet.
'Well, my mother-in-law is coming to visit us, and I don't want anything in the house to suggest she's welcome.'

Two Jews were facing the firing squad.
'Have you a last request?' they were asked.
'Yes,' began the first, 'I'd—'
'Ssh,' interrupted the second. 'Don't make trouble.'

Said the cannibal to his wife: 'I've had a bellyful of your mother.'

An Irishman, a Scotsman and a Jew were condemned to die in the gas chamber in America. Each was asked if he had a last request.

Said the Scotsman: 'I'd like a bottle of Bell's whisky.'

The Irishman said: 'I'll take a crate of Guinness.'

The Jew said: 'I'd like a piano.'

Half an hour later they opened the door. The Irishman and the Scotsman were dead, but the Jew was sitting there playing the piano.

'How did you manage to survive?' asked the doctor.

'Simple,' replied the Jew. 'You see, Tunes help you breathe more easily.'

Two Africans were sitting on the bank of a river. Suddenly, one let out a yell.

'What's the matter?' asked the first.

'A crocodile has just bitten off my foot.'

'Which one?'

'What does it matter? Those crocodiles all look alike to me.'

Then there was the man who knew to the hour and minute when he was going to die. The judge told him.

A blind man was sitting in the golf clubhouse at St Andrews, when Jack Nicklaus walked in.

'Is that Jack Nicklaus, the great American golfer?' he asked.

'That's me,' said Nicklaus. 'Glad to meet you.'

'It's always been my ambition,' went on the man, 'to play you at golf.'

'It's my privilege,' said Nicklaus. 'Just to make the game interesting, shall we have a little side bet for, say, 5p a hole?'

'I thought we'd play for £300 a hole,' replied the man.

'If that's the way you want it,' agreed Nicklaus. 'What time shall we tee off?'

'Midnight tonight,' said the man.

A wife came home and found her mother standing in a bucket of water, her fingers stuck in the light socket. The husband was standing by the switch.

'Hello, dear,' said the mother. 'Arthur has this marvellous idea for curing my rheumatism . . .'

'Your little boy is spoilt, Mrs Brown.'

'How dare you! He's nothing of the kind.'

'No? Wait till you see what the steamroller did to him.'

Three Scots stagger into a bar near closing time. One collapses legless on the floor. The other two order a double Scotch each.

'What about him?' asks the barman, pointing to the unconscious man on the floor.

'Nae mair for him,' says one. 'He's drivin'.'

'Mummy, why are we pushing this car off the cliff?'
'Shut up or you'll wake your father.'

Graffiti:
I'd give my right ear to paint like Van Gogh.

A Scots farmer, about to re-marry, was reminded by his friend: 'Your first wife swore she'd crawl out of her grave and haunt you if you ever took another woman.'

'Aye, that's so,' agreed the farmer.

'Aren't you just a wee bit scared?'

'Naw, naw – she'll have a long crawl . . . you see, ah buried her upside-down.'

'Mummy, are you sure this is the right way to make potted head?'
'Shut up and get back in the oven.'

During the war, an Irish pilot in the RAF crashed in Germany and finished up badly injured in hospital.

'I'm afraid,' said the surgeon, 'we're going to have to amputate your right leg.'

'If you must, you must,' said the pilot. 'But do me a favour – send the leg home to Dublin.'

'I'll see to it,' promised the surgeon.

A week later the surgeon told the patient: 'Bad news . . . we'll have to amputate your other leg.'

'I quite understand,' said the pilot. 'Please send the leg to Dublin.' The surgeon agreed.

A fortnight went by, and the surgeon told the pilot he would have to take off his right arm.

'Very well,' said the pilot. 'Now be sure and send it to Dublin.' Again, he promised.

Finally, the surgeon broke the news that the left arm would have to be amputated.

'Go ahead,' said the pilot, 'but remember—'

'Don't ask me to send it to Dublin,' broke in the surgeon.

'Why not?' asked the pilot.

The Kommandant thinks you're trying to escape!

Preserve wildlife – pickle a squirrel.

On a gravestone in Woolwich:
Sacred to the memory of Major James Brush, who
was killed by the accidental discharge of a pistol by
his orderly on 14th April 1831. Well done, good and
faithful servant.

'How did you puncture your tyre?'
'Ran over a whisky bottle.'
'Didn't you see it?'
'No, the man had it under his raincoat.'

Charlie was crying as he knelt in front of the three
tombstones.
'Relatives of yours?' asked a sympathetic passer-by.
'Yes,' said Charlie. 'This one is my first wife. She
died from eating poisoned mushrooms. And this is
my second wife. She also died from eating poisoned
mushrooms.'
'What about the third?' asked the passer-by.
'She died from a fractured skull. She wouldn't eat
the mushrooms.'

Graffiti:
Save a tree – eat a beaver.

Then there was the American tourist who thought Joan of Arc was the first French fry.

News flash:
French wine-growers fear that this year's vintage may be spoilt by a grape treaders' sit-in.

'Is that 999?' asked Paddy.
'No, this is 998 – you've got the wrong number.'
'Well, do us a favour – run in next door and tell them to send an ambulance. There's been a nasty accident.'

Sign in tailor's:
Order your winter coat now. Because of demand, we will execute all customers in strict rotation.

'Dad, I want a lifebelt.'
'Well, you can't have one.'
'All right, then – let Mum drown.'

On the tombstone of a hypochondriac:
See – I *told* you I was ill.

'Does your grandma still slide down the banisters?'
'We wound barbed wire round them.'
'Does that stop her?'
'No, but it certainly slows her down.'

Then there was the cannibal who got married and, at the reception, toasted his mother-in-law.

The insurance man had an outsize nose, and Mrs Rawbottom was terrified her young son would mention it when he came to the house. On the man's arrival, she sent her son out to play, just to be on the safe side.
'Come in,' she greeted the man. 'Have you time for a cup of tea?'
'Aye,' he replied. 'That would be nice.'
'Sit down and I'll pour it,' she said. 'Tell me – *do you take sugar in your nose?*'

I'd give my right arm to be ambidextrous.

Hear about the bionic man who was stopped doing 150 m.p.h. on the M1? He was fined £50 and dismantled for six months.

Two cannibals had just eaten a missionary.
'Not a very pleasant meal, was it?' said one.
'No,' agreed the other, 'but at least it was better than those meat pies they used to serve us at Cambridge.'

A wife had been nagging her husband non-stop all day. Before going to bed, their young son asked:
'Dad, how did you meet Mummy?'
'I took a thorn out of her paw,' growled the father.

Graffiti:
Death is nature's way of saying you must slow down.

Bluebeard on phone to Scotland Yard: 'How should I know how many people I've killed? I'm a mass murderer – not an accountant.'

'I think I'll commit suicide.'
'Good, but turn off the gas when you're through.'

'Forget the alimony,' said Henry VIII to his latest wife. 'I've a better idea.'

The lawyer was reading the will. 'To my dear wife, I leave my house, 100 acres of land and £100,000.
'To my son, I leave my Rolls-Royce and £30,000. To my daughter, I leave my yacht and £25,000.
'And to my brother-in-law, who always insisted that health is better than wealth, I leave my sun lamp.'

'If you were half a man you'd take me to the circus.'
'If I were half a man, I'd be *in* the flipping circus.'

'Mummy, can I play with Grandad?'
'No, you've dug him up twice this week already.'

A prisoner who was about to be hung complained to the priest: 'I haven't had my breakfast, Father.'

'That's nothing to do with me, my son,' replied the priest. 'I'm here only to look after your spiritual side.'

Then the warder came in, and the man said: 'I haven't had my breakfast.'

'That's not my responsibility,' said the warder. 'I'm here only to keep your cell clean and tidy.'

Finally, the hangman came in. 'I haven't had my breakfast,' exclaimed the man.

'That's nothing to do with me,' said the hangman. 'I'm here to see you don't get your dinner.'

'Joe, this diamond ring is lovely.'
'Shut up and keep running.'

A moment's silence for the Irishman who was a haemophiliac. He tried to cure himself with acupuncture.

Then there was the crematorium that bottled the ashes and sent them to New Guinea as Instant People.

A man was walking behind the hearse with an Alsatian on a lead and a long line of mourners behind.

'What happened?' asked a passer-by.

'The dog killed his wife,' someone explained.

The passer-by went up to the man with the Alsatian and asked: 'Do you mind if I borrow your dog?'

The man pointed behind him. 'Get in the queue,' he said.

From a parish magazine:
'The winner of the contest to guess the number of sweets in the jar was Miss Brown, who will travel to Majorca by air, spend two nights in a luxury hotel (all inclusive), and fly home via Paris without needing to spend a penny.'

Customer: 'Your dog seems to enjoy watching you cut people's hair.'

Barber: 'Not exactly. You see, sometimes I snip off a piece of the customer's ear.'

Song for Swinging Homicidal Maniacs:
'When you grow too old to scream, I'll have you to dismember.'

'Doctor,' said the man at the party, 'I'm so glad to see you. For some time, I've been having these pains round my heart, running all the way up to my neck. What do you think it is?'
'I'm afraid I can't help,' came the reply. 'You see, I'm a Doctor of Economics.'
'Really? In that case, tell me . . . should I sell my shares in ICI?'

Card in shop window:
'For sale, three maternity dresses, never worn, also expanding lady's suitcase, as new.'

'Mum, I've knocked the ladder down outside.'
'Well, don't bother me – tell your Dad.'
'He already knows – he's hanging off the roof.'

Judge: 'Why did you kill your husband with a bow and arrow?'
Wife: 'I didn't want to wake the children.'

Then there was the young boy at a party who was asked by the host how he got all those holes in his forehead.

'Learning to eat with a fork,' he replied.

Advice by a fuel economy firm:
'Use your head – burn wood.'

Sandy, the chief engineer, was buried at sea. When his body was lowered overboard, it was loaded down with pieces of coal.

Said his pal Hector: 'I knew fine where he was going, but ah never thought he would have to take his own fuel.'

Then there were the Irish tourists who wanted a day on the grouse moors. So a friendly farmer lent them two guns and four dogs.

Half an hour later they were back.

'What do you want?' asked the farmer. 'More ammunition?'

'No,' came the reply. 'More dogs.'

The foreman of the lumber camp put Casey on the circular saw. As he turned away, he heard the man say, 'Ouch!'

'What happened?' asked the foreman.

'I dunno,' came the reply. 'I just stuck out my hand like this and – *dammit, there goes another one!*'

'Like to hear the patter of tiny feet?' Ronnie Corbett's wife asked him in bed one night.

'Rather, darling,' he replied.

'Then go and get me a drink of water.'

And then there was the vulture with a sick expression on its face.

'What's wrong?' asked another vulture.

'I think I ate something fresh.'

'Doctor, my little boy here has swallowed a bullet. What shall I do?'

'Well, for a start, don't point him at me.'

Definition of a sadist:
Someone who's kind to a masochist.

'Tell me the worst, doctor,' said the man after his leg operation.
'Well,' he replied, 'the bad news is I cut off your good leg by mistake.'
'And the good news?'
'Your bad leg's getting better.'

Then there was the postman who went to hospital, complaining that a dog had bitten him on the leg.
'Did you put anything on it?' asked the nurse.
'No, he liked it just as it was.'

A Scotsman, an Englishman and an Irishman, sentenced to death, were allowed to choose between the guillotine and hanging.
The Scotsman chose the guillotine, but, just as the blade was about to fall, it stuck. According to tradition, he was released.
The same thing happened to the Englishman.
When the Irishman's turn came, he chose hanging, explaining: 'That damn guillotine doesn't seem to be working at all.'

Song for Swinging Undertakers:
'Painting the Shrouds with Sunshine'

There was an old widower, Doyle,
Who wrapped up his wife in tinfoil,
He thought it would please her
To stay in the freezer –
And, anyway, outside she'd spoil.

Missing, part-Persian cat, brown and orange.
Finder rewarded, dead or alive.

An undertaker, with an eye to business, called on an
elderly Scotsman and asked if he had thought of
making arrangements for the future. 'Naw, naw,'
replied the canny Scot. 'You see, I might get lost at
sea.'

Graffiti:
Get really stoned - drink wet cement.

'Doctor, I've got this terrible problem. I'm
currently in this show at the Palladium, but I get
terrified when I have to go out there in front of an
audience. You see, I can't sing, I can't dance, I
can't play an instrument – I can't do anything.'
'Well,' asked the doctor, 'why don't you just quit
the show and get out of the business?'
'But, doctor, I can't – *I'm the star!*'

Songs for Swinging Midgets:
'Thank Heaven for Little Girls'; 'I've Grown
Accustomed to Her Knees'; 'Little Things Mean a
Lot'

'How much are those kittens in the window?'
'A quid apiece.'
'How much for a whole one?'

Widow: 'That coffin you've brought for my husband
is much too big for him.'
'Don't worry, Mrs Brannigan – he'll grow into it.'

News flash:
Major Humphrey Prendergast, the big-game
hunter, famous for his slogan, 'Shoot 'em right
between the eyes!' was eaten last night by two one-
eyed tigers walking arm in arm.

Graffiti:
Free Wales – with every four gallons.

Headline:
Meat Shortage – Housewives Attack Ministers

'Why are you looking so gloomy, Charlie?'
'Twenty years ago,' explained Charlie, 'I asked a lawyer friend of mine what I'd get for killing my wife. He said that, with time off for good behaviour, twenty years.'
'I still don't understand why you're so gloomy.'
'Just think of it . . . today I'd be free!'

Doctor to patient: 'Are you on the National Health or would you prefer an anaesthetic?'

'Do you realize, Fred, that this room we rented is supposed to be haunted by a ghost that returns every year on this date at midnight to find a human sacrifice? Fred? *Fred?*'

Then there was the tiger who cornered Mr Aesop and ate him up.
'Go ahead,' said the tiger, 'try and make up a fable about this!'

'Doctor, I wish you would cure me of smoking in bed.'
'But lots of people smoke in bed.'
'*Kippers?*'

Then there was the sadist who thought his wife looked horrible in stripes . . . so he stopped whipping her.

Cannibal mother to child: 'I'd told you before – don't speak with someone in your mouth!'

Bridget was sympathizing with her friend on the death of her husband. 'I believe he fell from the Post Office Tower?'
'Yes,' came the reply. 'He dropped from the ninth floor.'
'Was it as high as that? I heard it was only the fourth.'

An absent-minded professor was conducting a class in zoology. 'Today,' he said, 'we'll dissect this frog and see what makes it tick.'
He took a paper bag from his brief case and out came a ham roll. 'That's odd,' he said, scratching his head, 'I could swear I've had my lunch.'

A very unlucky fellow, Schultz. He was about to die in the electric chair when there was a power cut. So they had to finish him off with a blow lamp.

A man bought a parrot and sent it to his grandmother for her birthday. 'How was the parrot?' he asked a few weeks later.

'Delicious,' she said. 'The flesh just fell away.'

'How long are you in prison for, Paddy?'

'Twenty-eight years. How long are you in for?'

'Twenty-five years.'

'Well, you'd better sleep nearer the door – you get out before me.'

'I've stopped our little boy from biting his nails.'

'How did you manage it?'

'Kicked all his teeth out.'

Graffiti:

Watership Down. You've read the book, you've seen the film – now try the stew.

Songs for Swinging Undertakers:

'After You've Gone'; 'Oh, What a Beautiful Mourning'; 'I'm Walking Behind You'

A husband and wife, both 91, stood before a judge, asking for a divorce.

'I don't understand,' he said. 'Why do you want a divorce at this time of life?'

'Well, you see,' explained the husband, 'we wanted to wait until the children died.'

A woman went into a pet shop to buy a bloodhound. The salesman produced a puppy for her approval.

'Look,' she said, 'that could be any breed. How do I know it's a bloodhound?'

'Rover,' said the salesman resignedly, '*bleed* for the lady.'

A man went into a pet shop and asked if they had any dead hamsters.

'Why do you want those?' asked the shopkeeper.

'I make jam out of them,' replied the man.

'You what?'

'I put them on my tulips.'

'Your *tulips*?'

'Yes, haven't you heard of tulips from 'amster jam?'

'Mummy, what's a cannibal?'

'Shut up and eat your brother.'

Then there were the two cannibals hunting for their dinner, when they saw a missionary on a bike. 'Look,' said one, 'meals on wheels!'

Graffiti:
Dracula, your Bloody Mary is ready!

'These are Grandma's ashes.'
'Oh, did the poor old dear pass away?'
'No – just too darn lazy to get herself an ashtray.'

The rabbi, recuperating in hospital after a major operation, was visited by the synagogue council. As they left his bedside, the chairman stayed behind and remarked: 'I'd just like you to know, rabbi, that the council had a meeting before coming to see you today.'
'By 13 votes to 7, we wish you a speedy recovery. There were 5 abstentions.'

'Hey, Jimmy,' said McGregor, 'remember that £5 cheque you gave me for drowning your cat?'
'What about it?'
'It came back this morning.'
'So did the cat.'

A British soldier called Jock wandered into a pub in Belfast one lunchtime. Four IRA men barred the way.

After a dust-up, the IRA men lay on the floor unconscious. Jock walked over to the bar, bought a pint and a pie, walked back, cut an ear off one of the IRA men, popped it in his pie, and ate it.

'What sort of soldier are you?' asked the barman curiously.

'Pie-and-ear Corps,' retorted Jock.

Rowbottom went to Blackpool for a fortnight's holiday. At the end of it, he died of a heart attack. His body was brought back to Manchester for the funeral, and one of his friends came to see him as he lay in the coffin.

'My, he looks wonderful,' he said to the widow.

'Aye,' she agreed, 'that holiday did him the world of good.'

A Jewish woman in London stipulated in her will that she be cremated and her ashes spread over Harrods.

'That way,' she explained, 'I'll be assured of having my daughter visit me at least twice a week.'

Then there was the Aberdeen millionaire who said on his deathbed: 'I bequeath my entire fortune to the doctor who saves my life.'

Hear about the man cutting his hedge with his new electric clippers? A neighbour popped his head over to say 'Peep-Bo', but he only got as far as 'Peep'.

A patient in a mental home was convinced he was God. Trying to humour him, a visitor asked if he really created the world in seven days.
'Leave me alone, I'm tired,' was the reply. 'I don't want to talk shop today.'

'Do you know what good clean fun is?'
'No, what good is it?'

A man rushed into a pub. 'Does anyone here own a large black cat with a white collar?' he asked. No reply, so he asked again, louder this time. Still no answer.
'Just my luck,' murmured the man. 'I must have run over the vicar.'

Then there was the dear old lady who couldn't get the hang of decimal currency. 'Why didn't they wait till all the old people were dead before introducing it?' she asked.

A man got on a bus, and the conductor said, 'You want a 20p ticket, don't you?'
'Yes,' said the man.
'You've had a row with your wife, haven't you?'
'I have,' agreed the man.
'And now you're going to hospital.'
'That's incredible,' said the man. 'I *do* want a 20p ticket, I *have* had a row with my wife, and I *am* going to the hospital. How on earth did you know?'
'Easy,' replied the conductor. 'You've still got the chopper in your head.'

Hear about the cannibal who wouldn't put a Franciscan missionary into the stew-pot because he was a friar?

Then there was the fancier who bought a racing pigeon, which, unfortunately, died after hitting a telegraph pole at 80 m.p.h. He says he's getting another pigeon, and, next time, will aim it slightly more to the left.

'That's Carruthers all over. Willed his body to science, and science is contesting the will.'

Comedian to heckler: 'If you're ever in California, I hope you'll come by and use my pool – I'd love to give you some drowning lessons.'

A Cork man emigrated to England, and got a job in a crematorium. He wrote home to his mother: 'I've got the most wonderful job in the world. I'm burning Englishmen all day and getting paid for it.'

Doctor: 'Did you drink your orange juice after your bath as I suggested?'
Patient: 'After drinking the bath, doctor, I didn't have room for the orange juice.'

And how about the drunk who wandered into a wake in Dublin? Instead of looking into the coffin, he lifted the lid of the piano.
'I don't know who he was,' he said, 'but, by God, he had a wonderful set of teeth.'

On his first day, the Army recruit was issued with battledress, beret, underwear, socks, boots and walking-out uniform . . . all of which fitted him perfectly. They discharged him for being deformed.

Then there was the plastic surgeon who dozed off in front of the fire . . . and melted.

Hear about the Londonderry man who said he would rather die than be buried in a Protestant cemetery?

'Mummy, you can go to bed now – Dad's locked up for the night.'
'Are you sure? It's a bit early.'
'It's true . . . the police just phoned.'

How do you torture a Scotsman?
Nail his feet to the floor and play a Jimmy Shand record.

From a hospital notice board:
'Dangerous drugs must be locked up with the ward sister.'

Then there's the latest cooking aid from Africa – the non-pan frying stick.

And how about the successful guillotine manufacturer?
He's up to his neck in orders.

'I know you wish I was dead,' said the mother-in-law, 'so you could stamp on my grave.'
'Not me,' murmured the son-in-law. 'I hate standing in queues.'

How about the wife with a nasty turn of mind? Her idea of pleasure was to grease the kitchen ceiling and watch the flies go mad trying to land on it.

'The blueberry pie looks a bit odd, darling.'
'Oh, dear, maybe I put too much bluing in it.'

Definition of mixed emotions:
A man seeing his mother-in-law backing over a cliff in his new car.

Hear about the masochist who likes nothing better than a cold bath every morning? So he has a warm bath every morning.

A man asked his bank manager for a loan.
'By rights, I should refuse your request,' said the manager, 'but I'll give you a sporting chance. One of my eyes is made of glass. If you can tell me which one it is, I'll grant you the loan.'
The customer looked at the manager's eyes intently, and then said: 'It's your right eye.'
'That's correct,' said the manager. 'The loan is yours. How did you guess?'
'Well,' came the reply, 'it appeared the more sympathetic of the two.'

How do you stop a cock crowing on Monday morning?
Eat him for Sunday lunch.

Telegram from Australia: BERT KILLED BY SHARK.
Reply from wife: SEND HIM HOME.
Further telegram from wife: MISTAKE. ONLY SHARK IN COFFIN.
Reply from Australia: NO MISTAKE. BERT IN SHARK.

Then there was the man whose hobby was parachuting. He took it up the day his plane caught fire.

'You know,' said one golfer to another, 'I always feel a bit guilty about playing on a Sunday.'
'I couldn't have gone to church, anyway,' replied the other. 'The wife had a heart attack last night.'

A man walked into a pub and announced: 'My dog understands every word I say.' The regulars looked sceptical, so the man suggested a small wager to prove his point.
After the regulars collected £10 from a whip-round, the man said: 'If I tell my dog to do something, and he obeys, I win the £10 . . . right?' The others agreed.
So the man picked up the dog, walked to the fireplace, threw it on the blazing fire, and said: '*Get off!*'

Then there was the man who was so paranoid he couldn't go to football matches. Every time the referee and linesmen went into a huddle, he thought they were talking about him.

Graffiti:
Help a nun kick the habit!

And how about the man in New Guinea who was condemned to death for cannibalism? On the day of execution, he rose, got dressed, cleaned his teeth and ate a hearty warder.

'Doctor, is a boy of ten capable of performing an appendectomy?'
'Of course not, madam.'
'Hear that, Chester? Now go and put it right back!'

Then there were the cannibals who got their first taste of religion when they ate a divinity professor.

'The chewing gum worked fine,' the old lady told the stewardess on leaving the plane. 'But, tell me, how do I get it out of my ears?'

'Daddy, I don't want to go to America.'
'Shut up and keep swimming.'

A man took his dog to the vet and said he couldn't get it to stop howling.
'No problem,' said the vet, giving the dog a hefty kick.
'That's great,' said the man. 'It's stopped. How did you do it?'
'Simple,' replied the vet. 'Hush Puppies.'

On a tombstone:
You wouldn't believe me when I said my feet were killing me.

'Why are you looking so miserable, Charlie?'
'Didn't you know? My wife died last week.'
'But surely I went to your wife's funeral three years ago.'
'That was my first wife. This was my second wife who died.'
'And to think I didn't know you'd married again. *Congratulations!*'

How about the efficiency expert who was being carried to his grave by six pallbearers?
Just as they got to the graveside, he popped up out of his coffin and shouted: 'If you'd put this thing on wheels, you could lay off four men!'

Wife to husband: 'Mother's made up her mind she wants to be cremated.'
Husband: 'Tell her to get her things – I'll be right over.'

Talking of cremation, a wife had her husband cremated and kept his ashes in an urn on the mantelpiece. When friends came to visit her, they would often unknowingly flick their cigarette ash into it.
One day as she was cleaning the mantelpiece, she picked up the urn. 'I don't know if it's just my imagination,' she murmured, 'but it seems to me that Walter's putting on weight.'

Graffiti:
You haven't lived until you've died in Welwyn Garden City.

The party of tourists were taken on safari into the bush. At one village the guide introduced them to a white man who was only 12 inches tall.
'Good afternoon, Carruthers,' said the guide. 'Tell the tourists about the time you told the witch doctor what to do with his bananas.'

'I want a coffin for my husband, who's just died.'
'Certainly, madam. I have one at £100 and one at £20.'
'What's the difference?'
'On the £20 one, there's a six-month waiting list.'

Sign at a cemetery:
Due to industrial dispute, graves will be dug by a skeleton staff.

When the actor died, there was standing room only at the funeral. Confided his agent to a friend: 'If he'd known he'd have an audience like this, he'd have died years ago.'

'I hear your husband had a post-mortem examination, Mrs Donnelly.'
'Yes,' she agreed, 'but not until he was dead. If they'd done it a bit earlier, they might have saved his life.'

On a tombstone:
Here lies Morris Goldstein.
Died August 9, as of September 1.

Then there was the girl who received a Valentine's Day heart from Christopher Lee. Still beating.

The Best Man went to jail for a long stretch just before the wedding. He was visited by the bride's mother.
'Daphne is very sorry you won't be able to be at the wedding,' she said. 'But she's asked me to tell you how much she and Peter are looking forward to seeing you at their Silver Wedding.'

Hear about the Irishman who confessed on his deathbed to three murders?
He got better.

'How are you doing?' Dracula asked the fisherman on the riverbank.
'Haven't had a bite all day,' complained the angler.
So Dracula bit him.

The cannibal on a flight to Britain was asked by the stewardess if he'd like to see the menu.
'No,' he replied, 'I'd rather see the passenger list.'

Do you know Dracula's favourite fruit?
Nectarines.

Then there was the cannibal on a diet. He only eats midgets.

'My sister thinks you're the funniest comedian in show business.'
'That's very sweet of her. I'd like to meet her some time.'
'You can't – we never let her out of her room.'

'You've got to help me, doctor.'
'What seems to be the trouble?'
'Some little blue men are living in my shoes.'
'So?'
'They won't pay their rent!'

A boy ran into a photography shop. 'My brother's being gored by a runaway bull!' he shouted.
'What am I supposed to do about it?' asked the owner.
'Put a new roll of film in my camera!'

'How do you mean your mother-in-law is vengeful?'
'When she caught rabies, she sat down and wrote out a list of people to bite.'

I wouldn't say she's a bad cook. But, when she makes soup, the Pygmies come from Africa to dip their darts in it.

A man was fishing off the end of the pier, when an onlooker fell into the sea. As he was coming up for the second time, the angler shouted: 'Next time you're down, will you see if my bait is still on the hook?'

An out-of-work ballet dancer in Dublin heard there was a job going at Covent Garden and decided to swim across.
Halfway over, he got cramp and started to sink. Luckily, a passing seagull saw his plight, dropped a rope and towed him safely to Britain.
After his audition at Covent Garden, the director asked him how he had travelled over. The dancer told his story.
'I'm sorry,' said the director, 'we can't take you on.'
'Why ever not?' asked the dancer.
'It's not our policy to employ pigeon-towed ballet dancers.'

Then there was the guru at the dentist who refused an injection. He wanted to transcend dental medication.

The chief whipcracker on a Roman galley tells the slaves: 'I've some good news and some bad news. Which would you like to hear first?'
'The good news,' chorused the slaves.
'Well,' says the whipcracker, 'you can have the rest of the day off, and as much food and drink as you want.'
'And the bad news?'
'Tomorrow your Emperor wants to go water-skiing.'

Then there was the Irishman who put his teeth in the wrong way round . . . and ate himself.

A policeman was trying to talk a man out of committing suicide by jumping in the Thames from London Bridge.
'That water's freezing,' he said. 'I'm married with six children. If you jump, I'll have to go in after you, then who's going to take care of my wife and kids? Now be a good fellow and go home and hang yourself.'

Then there was the man in the divorce court who claimed his wife kept shouting at him that he was driving too fast along the M1. To make matters worse, she swore at him while he was untying her from the roof-rack.

A deep-sea diver was walking along the sea bed, when he came across a young man dressed in blazer and flannels, wearing an Old Etonian tie. Pulling out his scribble pad, the diver wrote: 'What are you doing here?'
The young man reached for the pad and scribbled: 'Drowning, you idiot!'

A motorist ran into a police station and shouted: 'Come quickly, constable – I've just hit a student.' 'Sorry, sir, it's Sunday,' replied the policeman. 'You can't collect the reward till tomorrow.'

Hear about the man who died drinking a can of Longlife?

We were so poor my mother baked a lavatory brush and served it for dinner. Mind you, I thought it had rather a long neck for a hedgehog.

LORNE

The married couple were arguing over the breakfast table. 'You and your suicide attempts,' yelled the husband. 'Take a look at this gas bill!'

'Dad, can we have a dog for Christmas?'
'No, we'll have turkey as usual.'

'Sorry I'm late – my mother-in-law got burned.'
'Badly?'
'They don't mess about at the crematorium.'

Three men went looking for a bed for the night. The landlady said she could accommodate them on condition they didn't laugh at her son, who had no ears. The men agreed.
Next morning the first man came down for breakfast and told the boy: 'Always look after your teeth, son, or you'll end up with false ones, like me.'
The second man arrived and told him: 'Remember to keep your hair in good condition or you'll finish up bald, like me.'
Then the third man arrived. 'Take my advice,' he told the boy, 'and always look after your eyes. Otherwise, if you ever need glasses, you'll have nothing to hang them on.'

Graffiti:
Dyslexia rules – K.O.

'My mother-in-law was bitten by a poisonous snake in Africa.'
'Really?'
'Yes, it was horrible watching the snake die.'

Quasimodo went to this Jewish tailor for a suit.
'I want one of the sleeves to stop at the elbow,' he said, 'and I want one trouser shorter than the other. I want no lapels on the jacket, no pockets, and no turn-ups. How much will it cost?'
'Well,' replied the tailor, 'with all those extras . . .'

Think you've got troubles? How about the deep-sea diver coming up who passed his ship going down?

'Two pairs of No. 9 needles, please.'
'Taking up knitting, sir?'
'No, I'm a sword swallower on a diet.'

Hear about the termite that went into a bar and asked: 'Is the bar tender here?'

Then there was the frog that bequeathed its legs to Andre's Bistro.

And the bow-legged man being measured for trousers by a confused tailor. 'Just make them straight,' he said. 'I'll do the bending.'

Graffiti:
Insanity is hereditary.
You get it from your kids.

'Sorry to hear your brother died.'
'Yes – he fell off a scaffold.'
'What was he doing up there?'
'Getting hanged.'

Identical twins Fred and Charlie were always being mistaken for each other.
'But I got even with Charlie last week,' Fred told a friend.
'What happened?'
'I died and they buried him.'

A wife was visiting her newly-convicted husband in prison. 'Well, I'm afraid I must be going,' she said at last.
'What's the hurry?' asked the husband.
'Mother's giving a party for the jurors.'

Then there was the scientist who crossed a crocodile with a parrot.
It bit off his arm and said: 'Who's a pretty boy, then?'

'Try to be nice to mother when she visits us this weekend, Arthur, and fall down when she hits you.'

'Is that hand-knitted?'
'No, it came with my arm.'

Graffiti:
I'm a procrastinator because . . .
I'll tell you tomorrow.

'Why is your mother selling matches in the street?'
'Well, it's hardly worth opening a shop for half a dozen boxes of matches.'

'This is your last chance,' said the undertaker. 'If you haven't paid cash for your grandmother's funeral by next Thursday – *up she comes.*'

Then there was the beatnik cannibal who ate three squares a day.

'Has a lemon got legs?' the man in the pub asked his mate.
'Of course not,' came the reply.
'Then I've just squeezed the canary into my gin.'

As Fritz pushed his mother over a cliff, he said to his brother: '*Look, Hans – no Ma!*'

The screen was placed round the hospital patient's bed, and the nurse came in with a tape measure.
'What on earth are you going to do, nurse?' asked the patient.
'If you must know, I'm measuring you for a coffin.'
'But I'm not dead.'
'Sssh! Do you want to make a fool out of the doctor?'

'This is your captain. One of the engines is on fire, but there is no need to panic.'

'Who's panicking?' said Paddy. 'The fire isn't on my side of the plane.'

'Excuse me, madam,' said the motorist, 'do you own a black cat with a red collar and a silver bell?'

'Yes, that's my cat.'

'Well, I'm afraid I just ran over it. But, don't worry, I'll replace it.'

'Fine,' said the woman. 'Now about this mouse in the kitchen . . .'

'I've a confession to make,' said Monty to his partner Wolfie on his deathbed. 'I robbed our firm of £50,000, I sold secrets to our rivals, I had an affair with your wife—'

'It's all right,' interrupted Wolfie. 'It was me that poisoned you.'

'I'm afraid your husband drowned in a vat of Guinness at the brewery.'

'Was it quick and painless?'

'Painless yes, but quick, no. It wasn't till we pulled him out for the third time that we realized he was starting to drown.'

'What's this ranch called?'
'The Diamond Horseshoe Lazy Z Circle Y Bar M.'
'How many head of cattle are there?'
'Not many, pardner. Very few survive the branding.'

Two gin rummy addicts talking:
'I know you've been fooling around with my wife, but I still love her,' said one. 'Let's settle this in a civilized way.'
'What do you want to do?'
'We'll play one game of gin – the winner keeps my wife.'
'OK, but just to make it interesting – let's play for a penny a point.'

Then there was the man with two wooden legs who was trapped in a fire and burned to the ground. The insurance company wouldn't pay out . . . said he hadn't a leg to stand on.

Two snakes in the jungle:
Said one: 'Are we supposed to be poisonous?'
'Why?'
'I've just bitten my lip.'

'Mummy, I want a drink of milk.'
'Shut up and drink your weedkiller.'

A Rangers supporter was standing weeping bitterly at the top of a cliff, over which a busload of Celtic fans had just plunged.
'Why are you crying so much?' asked a policeman.
'There were two empty seats,' explained the fan.

'Dad, do you like baked apples?'
'Yes, why?'
'The forest fire's reached the garden.'

When the drunk rolled home, he asked his wife, 'Is that bottle of yellow stuff in the bathroom cabinet hair restorer?'
'No, it's glue.'
'No wonder I couldn't get my hat off in the pub.'

Nagged the golfer's wife, 'If you ever spent a Sunday with me instead of playing golf, I think I'd drop down dead.'
Replied the husband: 'Bribery will get you nowhere.'

The mother-in-law was sounding off. 'I'm fed up with the way you treat my daughter,' she told the son-in-law. 'When you're dead and gone, I'll dance on your grave.'

So the son-in-law arranged to be buried at sea.

A man called at the pet shop. 'Do you know what happened when I washed my hamster in detergent?'

'No – what?'

'It died.'

'I'm not surprised. Detergent isn't good for hamsters.'

'It wasn't the detergent that killed it – it was the spin-drier.'

A tailor found his partner bandaged from head to toe, walking on crutches. 'What happened?' he asked.

'You remember the yellow- and pink-checked suit with the narrow lapels we've been stuck with for years? Well, I finally sold it.'

'So . . . didn't the customer like it?'

'He loved it, but the guide dog nearly killed me!'

The moral of the story of Jonah and the whale is that you can't keep a good man down.

Then there was the cannibal chief who traded in his E-type jaguar for an F-type crocodile.

The condemned man was due to die in the electric chair for 17 murders. 'The date has been fixed,' said the priest. 'You're to die on Monday. Have you anything to say, my son?'
'Yes, Father – what a lousy way to start the week.'

'Mummy, can I go out and play?'
'Yes, but stay on the M1.'

Every morning the mother would beat her little boy over the head with a loaf of bread, saying: 'You naughty boy, you naughty boy!'
One day the next-door neighbour noticed she was beating him with a cake, saying, 'You naughty boy, you naughty boy!'
'What's the idea of hitting him with a cake?' he asked.
'Well,' she replied, 'it's his birthday.'

A man asked a butcher why he had human arms and legs hanging up in his window.

'We're a family butcher, aren't we?' was the reply.

Then there was the motorist whose wife had so many silicone operations he used her to polish his car..

McGregor was dying. He asked if a piper could be allowed into his hospital ward so he could hear the bagpipes for the last time.

The request was granted, and McGregor recovered. The rest of the patients died.

The sign in the junk shop said: 'Step inside and buy what your grandfather threw away.'

So Jackson stepped inside, and the first relic he found was his grandmother.

Then there was the actor who threw himself into the part of Abraham Lincoln in a new play, dressing like him and behaving like him in every way. On the way home from the theatre one night, he was assassinated.

Cut-price self-service funerals are the latest thing in Aberdeen. They just loosen the earth and you sink in by yourself.

Then there was the man who put a silencer on his shotgun because his daughter wanted a quiet wedding.

'Knock-knock.'
'Who's there?'
'The Boston Strangler.'
'Gladys – it's for you.'

The man phoned his doctor: 'It's my mother-in-law. She's lying at death's door. Can you come and pull her through?'

A moment's silence for the Human Fly at the circus that committed insecticide.

Said the doctor after examining the hippie: 'Take this three times a day with water.'
'What is it?'
'Soap.'

Then there was the angler who put his hand in a shark's mouth to see how many teeth it had. The shark closed its mouth to see how many fingers the angler had.

'I'd like to have a day off to attend my mother-in-law's funeral, sir.'
'So would I, Jones, so would I, but she's a picture of health.'

Dunlop inserted an advert in his local newspaper offering a £200 reward for the return of his wife's cat, no questions asked.
'That's a big reward for a cat,' said the clerk.
'Not for this cat,' retorted Dunlop. 'I drowned it.'

How about the Irish helicopter pilot who crashed? He thought it was a bit cold, so he turned the fan off.

Then there were the two Irishmen riding in a bus to the gallows. 'I'll get the fares there,' said one, 'and you can get them on the way back.'

Heard about the doors in the undertaker's labelled HIS and HEARSE?

'What are the chances of my operation being
successful, nurse?'
'Very good indeed.'
'How can you be so sure?'
'Well, nine out of ten people never regain
consciousness after the operation you're having.
You're the tenth – the other nine died.'

How about the drunk man in the hotel lobby who
bet he could whip anybody in the place? The
elevator man took him up.

'Daddy, what's a vampire?'
'Shut up and drink your blood.'

Uncle Syd a bad lot? He only saw the priest three
times in his life – when he was baptized, when he
was married, and when they hanged him.

Then there was the karate champion who joined the
Army. On his first day he saluted an officer and
killed himself.

And how about the drunk who threw himself out of a seventh-floor window?
'What happened?' asked a young woman in the crowd.
'Don't ask me,' replied the drunk. 'I only just got here myself.'

Graffiti:
You'll never be the man your mother was.

'Are you sure I'll recover, doctor? I heard of a doctor who was treating a patient for pneumonia, and he died of malaria.'
'Don't worry – when I treat a man for pneumonia, he dies of pneumonia.'

What do you get if you cross the Atlantic with the *Titanic*?
Halfway.

A woman woke up in the middle of the night.
'Milton,' she told her husband, 'there are burglars downstairs. I think they're eating the pot roast I made yesterday.'
'Why worry?' came the reply. 'As long as they don't die in the house.'

A specialist was called in to examine the seriously ill hospital patient. The patient asked the nurse to listen at the door while the case was being discussed with doctors.

'Well,' he asked later, 'what did the specialist say?'

'I couldn't catch it all,' replied the nurse, 'but I heard him mention that we'd find that out at the autopsy.'

A bus conductor in Chicago was sent to the electric chair for pushing an old lady off the bus to her death. Asked if he had any last request, he said he'd like a banana.

After he'd eaten the banana, they pulled the switch but nothing happened. They tried again and, in the end, had to release him.

'Tell me,' asked the governor later, 'how did you do it? Was it the banana that saved you?'

'Not really,' replied the man, 'I was just a bad conductor.'

Then there was the doctor who still used the old-fashioned methods.

'I'm afraid I'll have to change soon,' he told a colleague. 'It's getting harder and harder to obtain the leeches.'

And how about the Irishman who put RSVP on a suicide note?

'Mummy, should I put the cat out?'
'Why?'
'It's on fire.'

'Can't you cure this cold I've got, doctor?'
'Look, go home and have a hot bath, then stand around in a draught for an hour or two.'
'Will that cure my cold?'
'No, but it'll give you pneumonia – and I can cure pneumonia.'

The angler went to cheer up his old pal, who was dying. For half an hour he chatted away, and soon the invalid felt more like himself.
Suddenly, the visitor noticed the time. 'I've got to go,' he said. 'We've a match on. See you back on the river soon.'
On the way out, he banged his head on a low beam in the bedroom. 'Bloody hell,' he said, 'they'll never get your coffin through here.'

'How did Mrs McGregor's appendix operation go?' the nurse asked the doctor.
'Appendix operation? I was told it was a post-mortem!'

'I can't play archery anymore, Hilary.'
'Lose your arrows?'
'No, they're all stuck in Mummy.'

'Mummy, can I feed the cat birdseed?'
'Why do you want to do that?'
'That's where the canary is.'

A man went into hospital to have his leg off. Next day the doctor came round and asked: 'Well, how's the leg?'
'You should know better than me,' said the man. 'You took it off.'

Then there was the window washer who was cleaning a window on the thirteenth floor when he stepped back to admire his work.

And how about the psychiatrist who was driving along the road when he spotted a man lying by the roadside, who had been mugged, stabbed and left for dead.

'Tell me who did this,' he pleaded. 'Whoever is responsible needs help at once.'

'Before I flog you,' said the guard to the Irishman, 'what would you like on your back?'

'Plenty of grease,' replied Paddy.

After the flogging, the guard asked the Englishman the same question.

'I'm tough,' said the Englishman. 'I don't want anything on my back?'

Then it was the Scotsman's turn. 'What do you want on your back?' asked the guard.

'The Englishman,' replied the Scot.

'Dad, that girl over there rolled her eyes at me.'

'Well, just pick them up and roll them right back to her.'

Hear about the man who was invited to a conference on schizophrenia?

He had half a mind to attend.

First kid: 'Bang, bang, you're dead!'
Second kid: 'Zap, zap, you're sterile!'

'Mummy, baby threw all her clothes out of the window.'
'So?'
'She was wearing them at the time.'

'Unfortunately,' announced the ringmaster, 'Marco, the Human Bomb, can't be with us tonight. He's gone off on holiday.'

'Mummy, can I go in swimming?'
'No – there's sharks in there.'
'But Daddy's gone in.'
'He's insured.'

Songs for Swinging One-Legged Tap Dancers:
'I Could Have Hopped All Night'; 'Knee Up, Mother Brown'; 'Twenty Tiny Fingers, Fifteen Tiny Toes'

Then there was the Scotsman running round the *Titanic* as it was going down, shouting: 'Anyone want to buy a genuine diamond ring for £5?'

And how about the foolproof method of teaching a Scot to swim? Pin a £1 note to his trunks and throw him in the deep end.

'Were you wearing a red scarf when you came in?' the barber asked the customer.
'No, I wasn't.'
'In that case, I seem to have cut your throat.'

A well-known magician featured sawing a woman in half. One day he appeared with a new assistant, and a friend asked where the former assistant was.
'She's retired and living in Liverpool and Manchester,' he replied.

Sign in an undertaker's:
Our coffins carry a lifetime guarantee.

Graffiti:
Lockjaw means never having to say you're sorry.

A motorist, returning from a wedding with his wife and young son, was stopped by the police and breathalized. The test showed he had been drinking.

'I'm afraid you'll have to come down to the station,' said the Sergeant.

'Wait a minute,' said the man. 'I haven't had a drink all day. Try the breathalizer on my ten-year-old son and see what happens.'

So the Sergeant gave the boy a breathalizer, and this time it indicated that the boy had been drinking.

'It looks as if the apparatus is faulty,' admitted the Sergeant. 'Please go on your way.'

Which the man did, saying to his wife: 'I told you it was a good idea to give the boy a double Scotch before we left!'

Then there was the Chelsea fan whose team had been knocked out in the first round of the Cup by an amateur side.

He got on a train home, joining an old lady who had a compartment to herself, much to her obvious annoyance.

'Don't worry about me, lady,' said the fan. 'I'm cutting my throat in the first tunnel we come to.'

'Daddy, why is Mummy running across the field?'
'Shut up and reload the shotgun.'

Then there were the two men taking part in a
shooting tournament. 'Hey, watch it,' said one,
'you've just shot my wife!'
'Sorry, chum,' said the other. 'Have a potshot at
mine.'

Said the doctor to the patient: 'I'd give you the good
news first, but there isn't any.'

Wife to husband: 'I'm afraid, dear, we're . . . er . . .
no longer a two-car family.'

Then there was the man who fell asleep with his
head under the pillow. The fairies came and took all
his teeth out.

Hear about the Irishman down in the dumps who
tried to commit suicide?
He took fifty aspirins. After two, he felt better.

'Had a good Christmas?'
'A fairy-tale one.'
'How do you mean?'
'Grimm.'

Doctor to hospital patient: 'We'll soon have you out of here . . . one way or another.'

A Chinese waiter was very irritated by a Greek customer who always made fun of the way he said 'flied lice' instead of 'fried rice'. All week he practised, 'Fried rice . . . fried rice . . . fried rice.' Next time the Greek came in and smirkingly asked for 'flied lice', the waiter drew himself up to his full height and said: 'It's fried rice – *you Gleek glit!*'

Nurse to patient: 'So you've never had an injection? Snap! I've never given one.'

Then there was the man who received a Christmas card wishing him peace and prosperity. It was from Bomber Command.

Two youngsters stopped a woman in the street. 'If you give us 50p, my little brother will imitate a cat,' said one.

'What will he do?' asked the women. 'Meow?'

'No,' came the reply. 'He wouldn't do a cheap imitation like that. He'll eat a mouse.'

Neighbours to departing holidaymakers: 'Is there anything special you'd like us to save if your house burns down?'

'Mummy, Mildred ate a poisoned mushroom.'

'I'm busy.'

'Now she's fallen in the river and can't swim.'

'The mushroom would have finished her, anyway.'

Only a mother-in-law could give a present of a pair of towels, one marked 'Yours' and the other 'Its'.

A magician was doing his act at a mental home, when he was heckled by one of the audience to sing a song.

At last the magician stopped his act and said: 'I don't sing. I'm a magician. I'm Tilly.'

Shouted the heckler: 'We're all Tilly – give us a song!'

At the inquest the coroner asked the widow: 'Can you recall what your late husband's last words were?'

'Yes,' she replied. 'He said: "I don't see how they can make a profit selling this corned beef at 10p a tin."'

Two football fans went to Rome for a European Cup game, and were discussing where to meet later in the day.

'I know,' said one. 'Let's meet at the Vatican.'

'Fair enough,' replied the other. 'The lounge or the saloon?'

After just five months of marriage, Crocker was considering the Foreign Legion. But he couldn't think of a way to force his wife to enlist.

'I have this problem, doctor. I keep stealing things.'

'Have you been taking anything for it?'

A man went into a pub and complained to a customer: 'I was just going down to get a paper and your dog went for me.'

'That's funny,' came the reply. 'It won't go for me.'

A mother and baby were trapped in a fire, and the crowd below were shouting to the mother to throw her baby down, but she wouldn't.

At last an Irishman stepped forward and called: 'I'm a Rugby internationalist. You can safely throw the baby down – I'll catch it.'

So the mother threw the baby down. The Irishman caught it expertly . . . and booted it down the street.

A girl was intrigued to learn that her girl-friend was a twin. 'Do people have difficulty telling you apart?' she asked.

'Not really – my brother's got a beard.'

'Everyone makes me out as some kind of a nut, doctor. I want people to treat me as a normal human being.'

'Do you always wear a ring through your nose?'

'See what I mean – you're as bad as the rest!'

The mother-in-law went to have her face lifted, but the beauty salon said it would be cheaper to have her body lowered instead. Six feet.

'Mummy, can I play in the sand pit?'
'Not till we find a better place to bury Daddy.'

Then there was the woman who willed that her fortune be divided between her cat and her dog. Her parrot is contesting it.

'They have wonderful beaches in Spain. My wife and I had a marvellous time burying each other in the sand. Next year, I think I'll go back and dig her up.'

'Stop the car,' said the wife. 'I forgot to switch off the iron. The house might burn down.'
'No, it won't,' replied the husband. 'I forgot to turn off the shower.'

What do you get when you cross a watchdog and a werewolf?
A very nervous postman.

Hear about the man visiting a cemetery who came upon a magnificent marble mausoleum with the name ROTHSCHILD on it?
'Wow,' he said, 'that's what I call living!'

Sign in window of bankrupt store:
We undersold everybody.

When Private Robinson's father died, the Sergeant-Major lined up the regiment and abruptly announced the news, whereupon Robinson fainted. The Sergeant-Major was told to use a bit more tact in future. So, when Robinson's mother died some months later, he drew up the regiment again. This time he said: 'Those with one parent alive, take one pace forward. *Robinson – where do you think you're going?*'

How about the man who won a plastic bag of goldfish at a fairground?
'They look very nice,' he said. 'Aren't you going to fillet them?'

'Mummy, when are we getting a garbage disposal?'
'Shut up and keep eating.'

'More speed,' shouted the Captain, so the Slave-Master went to work with his whip on their backs. But one of the slaves keeled over and died.

Said the Captain: 'Right – whip 'em all.'

'But one of them's just died,' protested the Slave-Master.

'That's what I mean,' said the Captain. 'When somebody dies, you've got to have a whip-round!'

A seaman decided to send a surprise gift home to his wife. So he rang Interpol and told them to deliver a parrot that could speak seven different languages.

When he eventually arrived home, he found she had plucked the parrot and eaten it.

'You fool,' he shouted, 'that bird could speak seven languages.'

'Well,' replied the wife, 'why didn't he say something before I put him in the oven?'

Graffiti:
I can't help being an Atheist. It's the way God made me.

And as the surgeon said when he severed an artery: 'Aorta known better.'

As widow Murphy complained: 'All these people who knew my husband turned up at his wake. But not one of them would have come to it when he was alive.'

My mother-in-law is so stupid that when she went to the mind reader, she was charged half-price.

Hear about the psychiatrist in a small way of business?
He reads shrunken heads.

'What were the patient's last words, nurse?'
'None, doctor – his wife was with him to the very end.'

As the relatives gathered for the reading of the will, the lawyer tore open the envelope and read: 'Being of sound mind, I spent every penny before I died.'

Two drunks were weaving their way home. 'Won't your wife hit the ceiling when you walk in tonight?' asked one.
'Probably,' said the other. 'She's a lousy shot.'

What do cannibals eat for breakfast?
Buttered host.

The soccer fans were surprised when the new signing turned out to be half-man and half-horse. 'He's our new centaur-forward,' explained the manager.

As McPherson left his dying wife, he said: 'I must go off on business for a while, but I'll hurry back. If you feel yourself slipping away . . . would you mind blowing out the candle?'

Hear about the man who threw his mother-in-law into the crocodile pool at London Zoo?
He's been prosecuted by the RSPCA.

An impresario was approached by a man who said: 'I've an act that's really unique. All you have to do is put £50,000 in the bank for my wife, and I'll commit suicide on the stage.'
'Not bad,' said the promoter, 'but what will you do for an encore?'

Paranoid mugger: 'Hand over your wallet or I'll kill myself.'

'Tell me,' the prisoner asked his wife on visiting day, 'is the money still safely buried?'
'Couldn't be safer. They've built a 25-storey block of flats on top of it.'

Doctor: 'That bottle of liquor you're drinking is very dangerous. One drink and you could go blind. Give it to me and I'll dispose of it.'
'That's very kind of you,' said McSporran, 'but I've got this blind friend . . .'

Then there was the Aberdonian who found a pair of crutches in the attic, and went down and broke his wife's leg.

Said one cannibal to the other, sampling the stew: 'This sure tastes good.'
'It should do,' said the other. 'It contains health-giving vitamin Charlie Prendergast.'

Mr Brown wishes to thank the doctors and nurses
at the cottage hospital for their kind help in the loss
of his wife.

The bus conductress was charged with witchcraft.
'Tell me what happened,' said the judge.
'Well, your honour,' she replied, 'we got to the
terminus, and I said "All change." And, before I
knew it, I had a bus full of frogs.'

'You must take a complete rest,' said the doctor.
'What's your occupation?'
'Anarchist, doctor.'
'Well, don't throw any bombs for six months.'

'Mummy, I just swallowed my mouth-organ.'
'Be glad you didn't play the piano.'

Hear about the woman who was the toast of the
town?
She forgot to turn off her electric blanket.

As O'Hagen staggered home drunk in the early hours, he was greeted by his wife.

'How dare you come home in that state, when we're going to a funeral tomorrow.'

'A funeral? Whose?'

'Yours.'

Then there was the Irishman sentenced to death by guillotine. Just as the blade was about to fall, a letter arrived from the authorities containing a pardon.

'Put it in the basket,' said the Irishman. 'I'll read it later.'

'Madam, your husband's just been run over by a steam roller.'

'I'm in the bath. Slip him under the door.'

Two men were sitting on a park bench. 'I'm afraid to fly,' said one. 'Those aeroplanes aren't safe.'

'Nonsense,' said the other. 'Didn't you read last week there was a train crash and five hundred people were killed?'

'What happened?' asked the other.

'An aeroplane fell on it!'

A fellow went into a fish shop and asked: 'Have you a cod's head for the cat?'
'Why?' asked the man behind the counter. 'Are you doing a transplant?'

Is my mother-in-law revolting? When she went to a horror film the other day, Christopher Lee picketed the cinema.

A minute's silence, please, for the party of Irishmen who ran on to the pitch at the Coliseum to get the lions' autographs.

A missionary was captured by cannibals and popped into the pot. He was surprised to see the cannibal chief suddenly sink to his knees and lift his hands in prayer.
'Am I to understand you're a practising Christian?' he asked hopefully.
'Of course, I am,' replied the chief. 'And please don't interrupt me while I'm saying grace.'

'I'm feeling so much better, doctor,' said the witch in hospital.
'Splendid. You can get up for a spell this afternoon.'

Then there was the stork that couldn't tell the difference. It dropped half a ton of margarine on a maternity hospital.

And how about the masochist who goes home and likes to slip into something uncomfortable.

'Mummy, why does Daddy collect musical instruments?'
'Why do you ask that?'
'The police were round asking what he'd done with the lute.'

Nurse: 'Do you want a bedpan?'
Patient: 'Don't tell me you've got to do your own cooking here!'

'My client is alleged to have killed his wife,' pleaded the lawyer. 'He's supposed to have chopped her up in little pieces, leaving only a thumb sticking out of the suitcase. You may think he's a beast, a killer, but I don't see him that way. A sloppy packer, maybe . . .'

As the woman in the shoe shop said: 'Oooh, it's agony! I'll take them.'

'Mother, can I have a new dress for Easter?'
'Certainly not, Richard!'

Then there was the hospital patient who felt his case had the doctors baffled. They fixed a suggestion box to the foot of his bed.

'Mummy. I found this funny shell in the sand.'
'Drop it down beside your father.'

Hospital visitor: 'How's my husband?'
Nurse: 'Compared with what?'

'Miss Smith,' called the tax inspector, 'there's a woman here wanting a rebate. Get out the "You'll be lucky" file.'

'Sorry to hear your wife died,' said Jock.
'Not nearly as sorry as I am,' replied Sandy. 'She'd hardly taken any of those expensive pills I bought her.'

'Mummy, I was sent home from school.'
'Why was that?'
'The boy next to me was smoking.'
'What did they send you home for?'
'It was me that set him on fire.'

'You'll be a widow in a few days,' said the fortune-teller to the customer.
'I know that,' she replied. 'What I want to know is – will I get caught?'

'I've lost a pound note,' said Cohen, 'and I've searched every pocket except one.'
'Why don't you search that pocket?' asked a friend.
'Because if it's not there, I'll drop down dead.'

The husband was looking at the newspaper. 'For twenty years,' he read to his wife, 'this chap had two wives. I call that despicable, don't you, Moira – I mean Jean.'

'When I first came to this town,' boasted the man in the pub, 'all I had was the suit I stood up in, a pair of shoes with holes in them, and a stick over my shoulder with a red bundle on the end of it. Yet now I own half the town, including three cinemas, half a dozen supermarkets and three office blocks.'

'Amazing,' said a stranger. 'Tell me, what was in the bundle over your shoulder?'

'Twenty-seven million pounds.'

'Yes, our holiday had everything,' this chap told his mate. 'Quiet pubs for me, sunny beaches for the wife, sharks for her mother . . .'

'Mummy, guess what I was doing.'

'What?'

'Throwing peanuts in the pond.'

'That's not so terrible.'

'Yes, it is – Peanuts can't swim.'

Hear about the driver who managed to get rid of the persistent noise in the back of his car?

He let her sit in the front.

Fred was going to get his mother-in-law a diary, but changed his mind. 'She hasn't been looking at all well lately,' he explained.

'We haven't been out for years,' complained the wife.
'Well, where do you want to go?' asked the husband.
'How about the cinema?' suggested the wife. 'I hear they've talkies now.'

'I think,' said the husband, 'sending Junior to bed with no dinner is a treat rather than a punishment.'

'How do you mean your family is strange?' asked the doctor.
'Well,' explained the patient, 'take the time my brother tripped and fell down a well on his ninth birthday.'
'What about it?'
'When we lowered his birthday cake to him, he didn't even tug on the rope to say thanks.'

'Bert! On second thought, don't eat those mushrooms. Bert! *BERT*!!'

'There are no hairs on your coat again,' said the suspicious wife.
'So?' asked the husband.
'Who's this bald-headed woman you're carrying on with?'

'Mummy, you know that walking-talking-laughing-crying doll you bought me?'
'What about it?'
'It's just been sick.'

'How can I cure my wife's nagging?' the patient asked the psychiatrist.
'By tolerance, kindness, understanding, affection and stuffing an old pair of socks in her mouth.'

Wife to husband: 'You know the patio you've always wanted? Well . . . er . . . now you've got one instead of a garage.'

Then there was the man who took his wife to the zoo. He's popping back to see her next Wednesday.

'I've some good news and some bad news,' said the man to his wife.

'What's the good news?' she asked.

'I'm getting £70,000 severance pay.'

'And the bad news?'

'Wait till you hear what they severed.'

The young dentist had quite a struggle to extract a patient's tooth. When the patient recovered, the dentist asked him how he felt.

'Apart from the footprints on my chest,' he replied, 'you seem to have put my head back the wrong way round.'

A man had a pet eagle, and was training it for six months to do a special trick.

'Has it done the trick yet?' asked his friend.

'Yes, I let him off this morning and he flew off with my missus.'

Hear about the man who was prosecuted for cruelty by the RSPCA?

He bought half a dozen homing pigeons and moved house.

And don't forget the two newly ordained priests who went on the town to celibate.

Epitaph for a hippie:
Don't dig me, man, I'm real gone.

When O'Reilly died, the priest, who had never met him, delivered a complimentary eulogy over the coffin lasting nearly half an hour.
Finally, the embarrassed widow nudged her son and said: 'Have a look in the coffin and see if it's really your father in there.'

'Mummy, where's my scarf? Where's my skateboard? Where's my Stevie Wonder album?'
'Hang on – I've only got three pairs of hands.'

Said one cannibal to the other: 'We had burglars last night.'
'Really?'
'Yes, and they don't taste half as good as missionaries.'

'Daddy, can I have a shovel? Robin fell in the
swamp up to his shoelaces.'
'His shoelaces? Why doesn't he just walk out?'
'He fell in head first.'

A man was admiring his friend's bulldog.
'That's not a bulldog,' explained the owner. 'It was
chasing a cat and ran into a wall.'

And how about the man who took his dog to the vet
after it bit his mother-in-law?
'Did you have it put to sleep?' asked a friend.
'No – I had its teeth sharpened.'

Graffiti:
Cannibalism can damage your health.

'Dorothy, I told you this plane didn't have a
powder room.'
'Shut up and pull the ripcord!'

'I've a great new act,' said the impresario. 'He's a magician who catches a bullet between his teeth.'
'What's so great about that?' asked the club manager.
'He stands with his back to the marksman.'

A doctor made a clone of himself, but it turned out so ugly he pushed it over a cliff.
Next thing he knew the police had arrested him.
'You can't arrest me,' he said. 'I didn't kill anyone.'
'Maybe not,' replied the Superintendent, 'but we're taking you in for making an obscene clone fall.'

'Doctor, I'd like you to see my wife – I think she's round the twist.'
'What makes you think that?'
'She bought a hundredweight of steel wool the other day.'
'So?'
'She's knitting an electric cooker with it!'

A man woke up after an operation.
'We've managed to save one of your eyes,' said the doctor.
'Thanks very much,' said the patient.
'Yes, we'll give it to you on your way out.'

After the carpet layers had finished, they noticed a bump in the middle of the carpet.
'That'll be my cigarettes,' said the husband. 'I'll flatten them with a hammer.'
Soon after, his wife came in. 'I found your cigarettes in the kitchen,' she said. 'By the way, have you see the budgie?'

'Mummy, all the kids say I look like a werewolf.'
'Shut up and comb your face.'

How about the Irish masochist who took painkillers?

And the hit man who wanted to concrete a client into the motorway?
He couldn't get planning permission.

She didn't so much tip the scales at eight stone, as bribe them.

Woman in hardware shop: 'I'd like to give my husband enough rope to hang himself. How much will he need?'

Then there was the prisoner who lived rough during his escape. He went home to his wife.

And the wife who asked her husband to buy her a nice, shaded spot in the Garden of Rest for her birthday . . . which he did.
When her next birthday came round, she asked her husband what he intended to buy this time.
'Nothing,' he replied, 'you never used last year's present.'

How about the docker who beat a tortoise to death? He pleaded it had been following him about all day.

Said the judge to the condemned man: 'You'll die when you hear this one . . .'

The guest was astonished to see the nine-year-old knocking nails into the expensive dining-room furniture.
'Don't you find it expensive letting your son do things like that?' he asked.
'Not really,' replied the host. 'I get the nails wholesale.'

A policeman pleaded with a man not to jump from a tall building. 'Think of your wife and kids. Think of your parents,' he pleaded.

'I'm not married and my parents are dead. Life isn't worth living,' came the reply.

'Life *is* worth living,' said the policeman. 'Look – Liverpool are playing at home tomorrow.'

'I don't care – I'm an Everton supporter.'

'Then go ahead and jump!'

'Thank you, doctor, for curing my kleptomania. I don't know how I'll ever repay you.'

'My fee is adequate, Mrs Johnston. However, should you have a slight relapse, I could do with a Polaroid camera and a transistor radio.'

The lawyer was cross-examining the defendant. 'After you poisoned the coffee, your husband sat at the breakfast table and sipped it. Didn't you feel the slightest touch of remorse?'

'Only when he asked for a second cup.'

'Mummy, I hate Daddy's guts.'

'Well, leave them on the side of the plate.'

Then there was the woman who couldn't get her alarm clock to go, so she took it to a German watch repairer.

When she had left, he tied the clock to a chair in a darkened room and hissed at it: 'Start verking . . . Ve haf vays of making you tock . . .'

And how about the American millionaire who spent a fortune on an anti-nuclear shelter for his family in the Arizona Desert? Just as he walked in to inspect it, an Indian shot him in the back with an arrow.

And the Pakistani who, after he saw a road safety warning on TV to wear something light at night, bought a white raincoat, shirt, tie, shoes, socks and hat . . . then got run over by a snow plough.

Or the Irishman who died of asbestos poisoning and left instructions that he wanted to be cremated.

'You can have one request before you face the firing squad.'
'I'd just like to sing a song.'
'Go ahead.'
There were a million green bottles, hanging on a wall . . .'

The comedian was having a hard time from the woman in the front row, who didn't laugh at a single gag.

Asked why, she explained that her husband had died, and she wasn't feeling too chirpy.

'Then why didn't you give your ticket to a friend?' asked the comedian.

'I would have,' she replied gloomily, 'but they were all at the funeral.'

Outside a church:
'The preacher for next Sunday will be found pinned up in the side porch.'

The couple had been married twenty-five years. To celebrate, the wife suggested they enjoy a slap-up meal at home.

'Go into the garden,' she said, 'and wring a chicken's neck.'

'Not likely,' said the husband. 'Why take out on a chicken something that happened twenty-five years ago?'

And how about the Irishman who bought a pair of tortoise-skin shoes? It took him four hours to walk out of the shop.

The teacher was surprised to find only one pupil in the class. 'The others are throwing cats in the river,' she was told.

One by one the pupils came in, each giving the same excuse. When the last one arrived, the teacher said: 'Why are you late? Were you throwing cats in the river, too?'

'No,' came the reply. '*I'm Katz!*'

Then there was the barber who took premises near the hospital, so his customers could get a quick blood transfusion.

One man who was rhesus negative went in for a shave. Verdict: Suicide.

'What would you do,' the wife asked the errant husband, 'if you found me in bed with another man?'

'Do?' replied the husband. 'I'd shoot his guide dog.'

The German got a job as a holiday-camp Redcoat. On his first day he welcomed a party of holidaymakers: 'Good morning, holidaymakers! Please line up in twos. You will march to the dining-room, then you will march to the swimming-pool. From there, you will march to the dance hall . . . and from there you will march through Belgium, France, Holland . . .'

The cross-Channel swimmer came out of the sea at Dover and headed for the nearest refreshment kiosk.
'A jug of coffee,' he said.
'Certainly, sir. Milk and sugar?'
'It doesn't matter – I'm pouring it over my feet.'

Two men were talking about Stephenson, who had just died.
'He was a very clean person,' said one. 'He took ten showers a day.'
'So?' asked the other.
'In tribute to him, the entire funeral procession went through a car wash.'

The Irish driver got a job on a one-man bus. On his first day the bus crashed through the plate-glass window of a shop.
'What happened?' asked the inspector.
'I don't know,' replied a dazed Paddy. 'I was upstairs collecting the fares . . .'

The Chief Constable was also the local vet. One night the phone rang and his wife answered it.
'Is your husband there?' said an agitated voice.
'Yes – do you want him in his capacity as a policeman or a vet?'
'Both,' came the reply. 'We can't get our bulldog to open his mouth, and there's a burglar in it.'

Hear about the cannibal who turned vegetarian?
He went off people.

Psychiatrist to patient: 'When did you get this
feeling that nobody liked you . . . you ugly, boring,
dreary, objectionable little man?'

As the man explained when he sold his prize
Doberman Pinscher for just £20: 'It turned on my
wife the other day and killed her, and now I've no
further use for it.'

Cannibal mum to teenage daughter: 'If your father
could see you now, he'd turn in his gravy.'

News flash:
Eggs are going up this week. The hens have lost all
sense of direction.

A man went for a brain transplant and was offered a choice of two brains – an accountant's for £500 or a politician's for £10,000.

'Does that mean the politician's brain is superior to the accountant's?' he asked.

'Not really,' explained the surgeon, 'you see, the politician's has never been used.'

Judge: 'I've decided to give you a suspended sentence.'
Prisoner: 'Thank you, your Honour.'
Judge: 'Don't thank me – you're going to be hanged.'

FOR SALE: Smooth-running hearse. Body needs attention.

Cannibal wife: 'I don't know what to make of my husband these days.'
Friend: 'How about a hotpot?'

A funeral parlour in America has come up with a cheap line in funerals. They wrap you up in a plastic bag, leave you at the airport and let somebody steal you.

'I've some good news for you,' said the doctor to the patient. 'The operation to cure your deafness has been a complete success.'
'You *what*?' said the patient.

Hear about the psychologist who taught his dog to eat when a bell rang?
It ate the Avon lady.

Then there was the Irishman who was arrested after drawing £10. The drawing wasn't good enough.

King Charles was about to be executed. Asked if he had a last request, he said he'd like to take his cocker spaniel for a walk round the block.

'Aren't you a bit young to smoke?' the man asked the small boy.
'Oh, no. I go out with girls as well. In fact, I was out with a smasher last night.'
'Really? And how old was she?'
'No idea – I was too drunk to ask.'

The lady driver asked the mechanic: 'What sort of service do you suggest for this second-hand car?'
'A burial one, madam,' he replied.

'Mummy, I don't want to go to Australia.'
'Shut up and keep digging.'

'You look so worn out,' said the dying woman to her husband. 'Go out for a walk and get some fresh air.'
He came back an hour later, bursting with news.
'Guess who's just got engaged?' he asked.
'Who?' asked the woman, faintly opening her eyes.
'*Me!*'

'Does your wife cook best by gas or electricity, Charlie?'
'Dunno – I've never tried to cook her.'

Feldstein was shopping around for a coffin. His friend Cohen offered him a bargain one for £750. Then he discovered the same coffin for sale at £500. So he went back to Cohen to complain.
'Did it have a silk lining?' asked Cohen.
'I didn't look. I don't think so,' said Feldstein.
'You see – in six months you'll need a new lining!'

Cannibal to victim: 'What did you do for a living?'
'I was an associate editor.'
'Well, after tonight, you'll be editor-in-chief.'

'How long have you believed in reincarnation?' the
doctor asked the patient.
'Ever since I was a frog, doctor.'

Hear about the insurance company that offered a
'Now or Later' policy? While you're in this world,
it's a life insurance policy. In the next, you're
insured against fire.

First cannibal: 'How did the new missionary go
down?'
Second cannibal: 'Fine. We've ordered another one
for Christmas.'

Then there was the vampire who was overdrawn
fifty pints at the blood bank.

And the sun-crazed vampire crawling through the
desert, crying, '*Blood! Blood!*'

My wife finally broke our dog of begging at the table. She let him taste it.

'Mummy,' asked the little girl cannibal, 'is that plane up there good to eat?'
'Just like a lobster, dear . . . only what's inside.'

'I've a new trick,' said the magician, 'sawing a woman in half.'
'What's so new about sawing a woman in half?' asked the impresario.
'*Lengthwise?*'

Two cockroaches were discussing a new restaurant. 'The kitchen is spotless,' said one. 'The floor is sparkling clean. There isn't a crack on the walls – not a speck of dirt in the place.'
'Please,' said the other, 'not when I'm eating.'

The passengers in the plane heard this over the intercom: 'Good morning, this is your pilot. This plane is entirely automatic, so you are perfectly safe. Sit back and enjoy your ride. I repeat – nothing can go wrong . . . go wrong . . . go wrong . . . go wrong . . .'

She was only a cannibal's daughter, but she liked her men stewed.

'Does anyone in this submarine know how to pray?'
'I do.'
'Good, you pray. The rest of you put on escape lungs. We're one short.'

'I've good news and bad news,' the doctor told the Irishman in hospital.
'Give me the bad news first.'
'I've had to amputate your feet.'
'And the good news?'
'The fellow in the next bed wants to buy your wellies.'

McPherson received £10,000 for injuries in a car crash, while his wife received £2,000.
'How badly hurt was your wife?' asked a friend.
'Oh, she wasn't hurt at all,' replied McPherson, 'but I had the presence of mind to kick her in the teeth before the police arrived.'

Three men met St Peter at the Pearly Gates.
'What did you do in life?' St Peter asks one.
'I was a school-teacher,' came the reply.
'Sorry, we've too many in here already.'
The same thing happened to the doctor.
'I don't suppose you'll want me, either,' said the
third man. 'I was a psychiatrist.'
'You're just the man we need,' said St Peter. 'God
thinks he's Margaret Thatcher.'

The explorer was just about to be boiled by
cannibals. In desperation he flicked his lighter and
it burst into flame.
'Look, magic!' cried the explorer.
'It sure is,' said the cannibal chief. 'That's the first
time I ever saw a lighter work first time.'

Then there was the man who read in the paper that
nicotine in cigarettes caused cancer in rats and
mice. So he put his cigarettes on the top shelf where
the rats and mice couldn't get at them.

Sign in an undertaker's:
'Drive carefully – we can wait.'

'I've two questions to ask you, doctor.'
'What's the first question?'
'Could I possibly be in love with an elephant?'
'Of course not. What's the second question?'
'Do you know anyone who wants to buy a very large engagement ring?'

The drunk arrived at the Registry Office in a happy mood. 'My wife had twin sons this morning, gentlemen,' he said, 'and I want to register them, please.'
'Certainly, sir,' replied the Registrar, 'but why did you say "gentlemen"? There's only myself here.'
'Is that so?' said the drunk. 'In that case, I'd better go back and have another look.'

Policeman: 'I've got a hunch, sir.'
Inspector: 'So I've noticed. You must learn to keep your shoulders back.'

According to Woody Allen, after six years of marriage he and his wife pondered whether to take a vacation or get a divorce. They decided that a trip to Bermuda is over in two weeks, but a divorce is something you always have.

Then there was the psychoneurotic Robin Hood. He steals from the rich, but keeps it.

And how about the man whose cat was run over by a steamroller?
He didn't say anything . . . just stood there with a long puss.

'Should chips be eaten with the fingers?' the dinner guest asked the cannibal chief.
'No,' he replied. 'The fingers should be eaten separately.'

'Waiter, the roof's leaking.'
'Are you sure, sir?'
'Well, it's taken me three hours to drink my soup.'

Newspaper headline:
BARBECUE OF SENIOR CITIZENS A BIG SUCCESS.

A neurotic builds castles in the air.
A psychotic lives in them.
A psychiatrist collects the rent.

The party of tourists stopped at a farmhouse which advertised lunches. They were given a meal of fresh eggs, potatoes in their jackets and lovely lean rashers.
On the way out they saw a pig limping with a bandage round its leg. 'Did it have an accident?' asked one of the tourists.
'Not at all,' replied the farmer. 'You wouldn't expect us to kill a whole pig just for you?'

The foursome was heading down the sixth hole, when Charlie, aged 87, dropped down dead in a bunker of heart failure.
His partner, Fred, all of 83, was telling the story at the eighteenth hole later.
'It was awful,' he said. 'Charlie snuffed it at the sixth, when we were two down. 'It wasn't so much we were losing, but it was terrible playing in – picking up Charlie, hitting a shot, picking up Charlie, hitting a shot . . .'

On a church noticeboard:
Ask about our pray-as-you-go plan.

Two fishermen were talking in the harbour.
'See that chap over there?' said one. 'He was a great shark man . . . used to stick his arm down the shark's throat. Called him "Fearless" in those days.'
'What do they call him now?'
'Lefty.'

'You're late,' said one frog to the other.
'Yes, I got stuck in somebody's throat.'

Newsflash:
Amy Turtle will not be appearing in Crossroads tonight. She rolled over on her back and can't get up.

'I think my MP is coming round in favour of capital punishment.'
'What makes you say that?'
'He hanged his wife yesterday.'

How about the Glasgow pub that advertised for dwarf barmen . . . for serving customers who drink themselves under the table.

Epitaph to an auctioneer:
Going, going, GONE!

'What do you do here about sex?' the American
tourist asked the old lady on the Outer Hebrides.
'Up here about sex we have our tea,' she replied.

Psychiatrist to patient: 'Just in case the medical
jargon has confused you – you're a nutter.'

Tough luck on the skeleton who couldn't go to the
dance. He had no body to go with.

Then there was the Irishman who thought his wife
was dying. So he moved her into the living-room.

'I'm afraid your wife has rigor mortis,' said the
doctor after his visit.
'Is that serious?' asked the husband.
'Well, let's just say she'll feel a little stiff in the
morning.'

Sign in hotel:
'Please don't smoke in bed. We don't want you to make an ash of yourself.'

'What did you operate on that man for?' the medical student asked the surgeon.
'Five thousand dollars.'
'I mean – what did he have?'
'Five thousand dollars.'

'Dad, what makes children become delinquent?'
'Shut up. Pour yourself another drink and deal.'

Lastly, did you hear about the professor who crossed a Jersey cow with a masochist?
He got cream that whips itself.